20-Minute Crafts: Beading

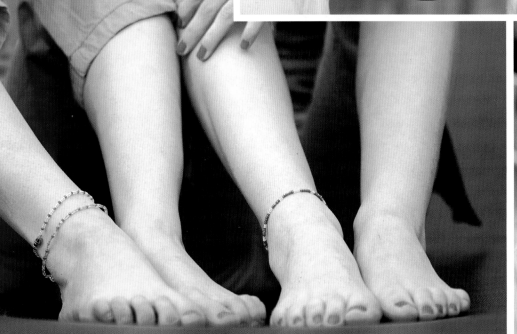
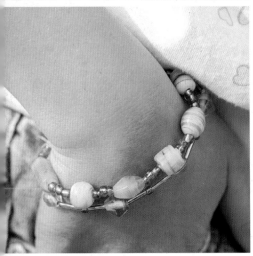

20-Minute Crafts: Beading

Katherine Stull

HANDS ON
Crafts for Kids®

Sterling Publishing Co., Inc. New York

A Sterling/Chapelle Book

Chapelle, Ltd.
  P.O. Box 9252, Ogden, UT 84409
  (801) 621-2777 • (801) 621-2788 Fax
  e-mail: chapelle@chapelleltd.com
  Web site: www.chapelleltd.com

Library of Congress Cataloging-in-Publication Data available

Stull, Katherine.
 20-minute crafts : beading / Katherine Stull.
     p. cm.
 "A Sterling/Chapelle Book."
 Includes index.
 ISBN 1-4027-2429-2
 1. Beadwork. I. Title: Twenty minute crafts. II. Title.

TT860.S79 2006
745.58'2--dc22

                                                    2005021665

10 9 8 7 6 5 4 3 2 1
Published by Sterling Publishing Co., Inc.
387 Park Avenue South, New York, NY 10016
©2006 by Katherine Stull
Distributed in Canada by Sterling Publishing
c/o Canadian Manda Group, 165 Dufferin Street
Toronto, Ontario, Canada M6K 3H6
Distributed in the United Kingdom by GMC Distribution Services,
Castle Place, 166 High Street, Lewes, East Sussex, England BN7 1XU
Distributed in Australia by Capricorn Link (Australia) Pty. Ltd.
P.O. Box 704, Windsor, NSW 2756, Australia
Printed in China
All Rights Reserved

Sterling ISBN 1-4027-2429-2

  For information about custom editions, special sales, premium and corporate purchases, please contact Sterling Special Sales Department at 800-805-5489 or specialsales@sterlingpub.com

Want to be part of the crowd, yet stand out on your own? Is it important for you to be able to express yourself? **20 Minute Crafts: Beading** offers you all these things along with a promise for a lot of fun.

Accessorizing your clothes and bedroom are a couple of ways to make a statement about who you are. However, you don't have to search the malls for just the right jewelry and room decorations. Why not be creative and design your own? Use the creative energy that you have been storing away.

Learn how to make fantastic chokers and funky bracelets like those in your favorite stores, only cooler! You're going to make them fit your personal style, using beads and cords of your choice.

This book is just the beginning. You're in for a treat. Get ready to find out how much fun and how easy it is to make jewelry and room decorations that express the real you. The hardest part will be choosing which beads and stringing materials to use. So, pick a project and let's go!

Adults can share in the fun of jewelry making with the young people in their life by tuning in to Beads, Baubles, and Jewels on your local PBS station. This program promises education, inspiration, and personal expression for the entertainment of beginners, as well as experienced beaders.

Chapter One - Jewelry

Chapter Two - Accessories

Glossary of Beads

There are more types of beads than you can imagine. They can be found in a multitude of colors, shapes, and sizes. Beads are usually measured in millimeters (mm).

• Bicone beads have a cone shape on each end.

• Bugle beads, available in plastic or glass, are tube-shaped and are available in various lengths.

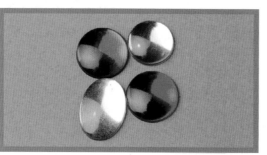

• Cabochons are made from stone or glass that is cut with a flat back and a domed top.

• Charms are available in many styles: alphabet, feathers, hearts, stars, butterflies, and much more.

• E beads are large seed beads up to 4mm.

• Faceted crystal beads can be plastic or glass. They have many cuts on the sides to create a diamond effect with flash and sparkle.

• Filigree or embossed beads are textured or embossed with a raised design.

• Gemstone chip beads are irregular-shaped pieces of gems like turquoise, quartz, jade, amber, amethyst, and more. They have a hole drilled in the center for stringing.

• Metal beads are available in various finishes like gold, silver, and copper and come in different shapes and sizes.

• Metal spacers, or rondelles, are ring-shaped beads available in many shapes and sizes. They are used to add interest to a design.

• Novelty beads are available in many styles: alphabet, hearts, stars, charms, ladybugs, butterflies, and much more.

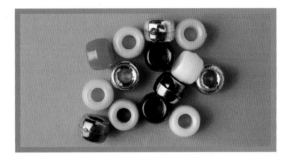

• Pony beads are short, cylindrical, plastic or glass beads with large holes.

• Rocaille beads are lined with silver to give a shiny, mirror-like effect.

• Seed beads are tiny beads available in different sizes and colors.

Glossary of Stringing Materials

There are several things to keep in mind when choosing a stringing material for your necklace or bracelet. Consider how flexible the piece needs to be. Will it be getting every-day wear and tear? A bracelet generally needs to be more flexible than a necklace. Also check the hole size of the beads. Use a stringing material that fills as much of the hole as possible, but keep in mind that some designs may need the stringing material to pass through the hole more than once. Use a large-eyed needle for very thin threads and wires.

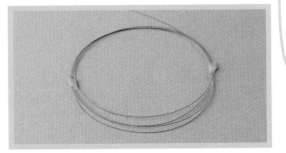

- Beading thread is thin and pliable. It is usually clear and may be used for illusion designs. It can be cut with sharp scissors.

- Beading wire is composed of very fine wires twisted or braided together and covered with a smooth plastic or nylon coating. It comes in a number of colors, but silver is the most common color used. There are a wide variety of diameters from .5mm or smaller for seed beads to .24mm for large-holed metal and glass beads. Wire cutters are needed to cut beading wire.

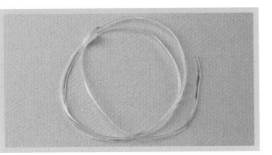

- Elastic cord, or stretch cord, is most often used for stretchy bracelets. It is available in clear or with a colored cotton finish. For seed beads, use cord that is .5mm or smaller. For large glass beads, use a 1mm cord.

• Hemp beading twine comes in a variety of thicknesses. It softens as it is worn.

• Leather, suede, and satin lacing or cords are available in several thicknesses and colors. They work well with large-holed beads.

• Memory wire is a steel spring wire used for coil bracelets, chokers, and rings. It retains its shape and is sold by the loop or in continuous loops.

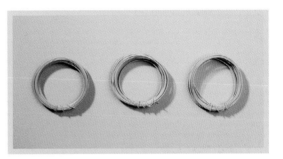

• Plastic-coated wire is used to make loops or to decoratively wrap beads. The smaller the gauge number, the thicker the wire. The thickest wire is 16-gauge wire, and 24-gauge wire is the thinnest.

• Ribbon in narrow widths works best. Choose a ribbon that has finished edges so that it does not fray when passing through the beads.

Glossary of Findings

Findings are the parts that link beads or finish off a necklace, a bracelet, or earrings.

• Crimp beads and crimp tubes are small metal beads that can be flattened or crimped into a tight roll with certain types of pliers. They are used instead of knots when stringing beads onto flexible beading wire.

• Crimp clasps, cord ends, and cord caps are used to attach cord or lacing to a clasp.

• Earring parts are available in various styles. Ear hooks and lever-back styles are popular.

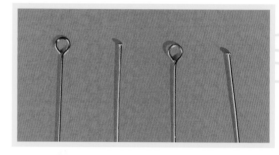

• Eyepins and headpins are lengths of heavy wire with a loop or flat head at one end. They are available in different colors and lengths.

• Jump rings are used to connect things. They come in a variety of sizes. They are split at one spot so that they can be opened and closed.

• Key rings are large rings that are split so that keys can be slipped onto the ring.

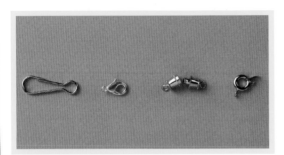

• Lanyard, lobster claw, barrel, and spring ring are the most popular styles of clasps to use for finishing off a necklace. They all open and close to allow you to take the necklace or bracelet off and on.

Helpful Tips

• **Place a bead mat or rough towel on your work area before spreading out all your materials. This helps to prevent beads from rolling everywhere when dropped.**

• **Use a bead board to organize and place your beads in the pattern you want before stringing them.**

• **Lay out all the materials you will need before starting your projects, including necessary tools and glue.**

• **When designing a bracelet, measure it on your wrist. If the bracelet is too small or too large, beads may be added or removed as needed.**

• **Cut wire, leather, cord, etc., a little longer than you think you will need. Extra length is simply trimmed off when finished. If the length is too short, restringing will be necessary.**

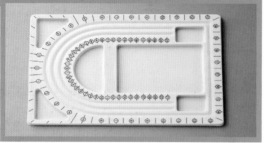

• Bead board, mat, or a rough surface so beads will not roll everywhere when dropped.

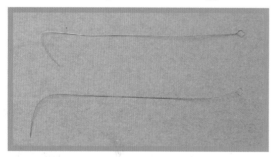

• Beading needles are used when working with very thin wire or threads. They should have a large eye for the stringing material to pass through.

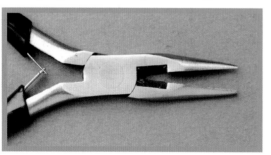

• Chain nose pliers are the all-purpose pliers. They can be used to make 90° angles, open and close jump rings, and to hold loops while wrapping. They can also be used for a simple flat crimp. There are also special crimping pliers, which crimp using two steps.

• Jewelry glue can be used to give extra security to knots, beads, or crimp beads and tubes at the ends of a bracelet or necklace. Use a clear glue that is recommended for beads and jewelry.

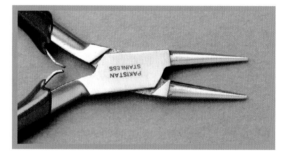

• Round nose pliers are used to make small loops with the tip of the jaws. The backs of the jaws are used to make large loops.

• Scissors are needed to cut stringing materials. Do not use scissors to cut wire; it will ruin the blades. Make sure your scissors are sharp.

• Wire cutters are used to cut wires and findings.

How to tie an overhand knot:

To tie an overhand knot, make a small loop at one end of the beading wire, elastic cord, or nylon cord, leaving a short "tail." Thread the tail through the loop and pull it tightly to form a knot.

How to tie a double knot:

To tie a double knot, simply tie an overhand knot twice.

How to crimp:

Place the crimp bead/tube inside the jaws of your chain nose pliers and squeeze hard to flatten. The word "crimp" in the instructions just means to squeeze hard to flatten and hold the wire on the string.

Note: If the instructions call for crimping, you can substitute knots; and if instructions call for knotting, you can crimp instead.

How to attach a clasp using a crimp bead or crimp tube:

String one crimp bead/tube onto the beading wire or nylon cord, then thread the wire/cord through the ring on the clasp and back through the crimp bead/tube. Crimp the bead/tube and either trim the wire/cord ends or thread the wire/cord ends back through several beads.

How to attach a clasp using an overhand knot:

Thread the end of the beading wire, elastic cord, or nylon cord through the ring on one side of the clasp and tie the wire/cord in a double knot just below the clasp. Repeat for the remaining side of the clasp. Place a dab of glue on the knots. Let dry.

How to attach an end cap:

There are several kinds of end caps. The most common one is a wire coil with a loop on the end. To attach a wire coil to a leather cord, place a dab of glue on one end of the cord. Slip the cord inside the coil and use chain nose pliers to crimp the first couple of rings. Let the glue dry.

How to open and close jump rings:

Jump rings are little circles of metal with an opening. To keep their strength and to not break them, it is important to open and close them correctly. The easiest way to use them is to use two sets of pliers. To open, hold the ring on each side of the opening with a set of pliers and twist one side away from you. To close, hold one side and twist the other side back to meet it to close the space. You should not pull the jump ring apart.

Chapter One - Jewelry

Simple Seed Bead Ankle Bracelets

by ALI RUSS

by ALI RUSS

You Will Need

To make each ankle bracelet:

- Seed beads in assorted colors
- .015" beading wire
- (2) Crimp beads
- Barrel clasp
- Chain nose pliers
- Wire cutters

Step 1

Cut a length of beading wire to equal the measurement of your ankle plus 4". String one crimp bead onto the wire, then thread the wire through the ring on one side of the clasp and back through the crimp bead as shown in **Diagram A** below. Crimp the bead.

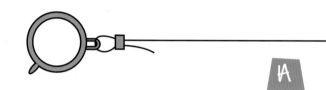

Step 2

Decide on a beading pattern for your ankle bracelet. Even patterns have a set design, while random patterns have a varied design without a standard look. Either pattern can be designed by color, by bead shape, or by the number of beads. String the beads onto the wire to the length you need.

Step 3

String the remaining crimp bead onto the wire, then thread the wire through the ring on the other side of the clasp and back through the crimp bead. Crimp the bead and trim off the wire ends.

Step 4

Fasten the clasp.

Note

When making ankle bracelets, use wire to make them a little stiffer. This will allow them to retain their shape rather than conforming to the shape of the ankle.

18

Variation

Combine seed beads with other beads such as mini bugle beads.

Elegant Satin Ribbon & Pearl Choker

by KRISTINE RUSS

You Will Need

- (38) White faux pearls
- (16") .015" beading wire
- (24") ¼"-wide black satin ribbon
- (2) Crimp tubes
- (2) Jump rings
- Chain nose pliers
- Wire cutters

Step 1

String one crimp tube onto the beading wire, then thread the wire through one of the jump rings and back through the crimp tube as shown in **Diagram A** below. Crimp the tube.

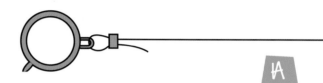

Step 2

String the pearls onto the wire.

Step 3

String the remaining crimp tube onto the wire, then thread the wire through the remaining jump ring and back through the crimp tube. Crimp the tube and trim off the wire ends.

Step 4

Fold the ribbon in half and thread it through one of the jump rings. Loop the ribbon through itself to attach it to the jump ring. Determine the length you need, then thread the ribbon through the remaining jump ring and loop through itself again. Tie the ribbon ends into a bow.

Variation

Ribbon colors are interchangeable to match any outfit. Simply slip off the existing ribbon and attach a new one.

Beaded Choker

by ANNA RUSS

You Will Need

- (15) Silver star beads
- (90) Black E beads
- Memory wire choker
- Chain nose pliers
- Wire cutters

Step 1
Make a small loop at one end of the wire choker. You may need to have an adult help you bend the memory wire.

Step 2
String six E beads and one star bead onto the wire choker.

Step 3
Repeat Step 2 to the length you need.

Step 4
If necessary, trim the remaining end of the wire choker to the length you need, then make a small loop to match the loop at the opposite end of the choker.

Variation
Change the appearance of your choker simply by using assorted colors of beads separated by heart beads.

Braided Seed Bead Bracelet

by ALI RUSS

Step 1

Cut the elastic cord into three equal lengths. Tie the cords together at one end, using a double knot. Place a dab of glue on the knots. Let dry.

Step 2

String a single color of seed beads onto one of the cords, leaving a 2" tail. Temporarily wrap a small piece of tape around the end of the cord to keep the beads from falling off.

Note: If you have trouble stringing beads on the cord. Use a fine beading needle.

Step 3

Repeat Step 2 with the remaining two colors of seed beads.

Step 4

Loosely braid the strands of beads, keeping them flat and untwisted. Check to make sure the bracelet fits your wrist. If necessary, loosen or tighten the braid to adjust the length.

Step 5

Carefully remove the tape from the ends of each strand. Tie the cord ends together, using a double knot. Secure with glue as in Step 1. Let dry.

Step 6

Tie the cords from both ends together, using a double knot. Trim off the cord ends and place a dab of glue on the knots. Let dry.

You Will Need

- (3) Seed beads in coordinating colors
- (45") .032" elastic cord
- Jewelry glue
- Tape

Variation

Create a colorful pattern with the beads instead of using only one color on each strand.

Clear Crystal Bracelet

by SARAH STULL

You Will Need

- (10) Clear crystal, flat triangular beads
- (30) Clear crystal E beads
- (10") .032" clear elastic cord
- Jewelry glue

Step 1

Tie a knot at one end of the elastic cord, using a double knot. Place a dab of glue on the knots. Let dry.

Step 2

String one flat bead and three E beads onto the cord.

Step 3

Repeat Step 2 to the length you need.

Step 4

Repeat Step 1 at the opposite end of the cord.

Step 5

Tie the cord ends together, using a double knot. Trim off the cord ends and place a dab of glue on the knots. Let dry.

Variation

Change the appearance of your bracelet by simply varying the pattern between small and large beads. Experiment with different sizes and colors of beads.

Semiprecious Stone Nugget Bracelet

by SARAH STULL

You Will Need

- (20–25) Semiprecious stone chip beads
- (25–29) Clear seed beads
- (50–58) Black seed beads
- Flexible beading needle
- (⅓ yd.) Elastic cord
- Craft glue
- Tape

Step 1

Tightly wrap a small piece of tape around one end of the elastic cord to keep the beads from falling off. Tie an overhand knot in the cord, just above the tape.

Step 2

Thread the cord through the needle. String one semiprecious stone chip, one black seed bead, one clear seed bead, and one black seed bead onto the cord.

Step 3

Repeat Step 2 to the length you need. Remove the needle.

Step 4

Tie an overhand knot at the end of the cord and carefully remove the tape from the other end. Tie both cord ends together, using a double knot. Trim off the cord ends and place a dab of glue on the knots. Let dry.

Variation

Choose any type of semi-precious stones from agate to turquoise.

Matching Memory Wire Bracelet & Ring

by ANNA RUSS

Step 1
Make a small loop at one end of the memory wire. You may need to have an adult help you bend the memory wire.

Step 2
String two turquoise, one royal blue, and one pink E bead onto the wire.

Step 3
Repeat Step 2 to the length you need. End with two turquoise E beads.

Step 4
If necessary, trim the remaining end of the wire to the length you need, then make a small loop to match the loop at the opposite end of the wire.

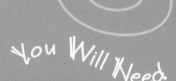

You Will Need

To make one bracelet:
- (48) Pink E beads
- (48) Royal blue E beads
- (98) Turquoise E beads
- (3) Coils of memory wire for bracelets
- Chain nose pliers
- Wire cutters

To make one matching ring:
- (7) Pink E beads
- (7) Royal blue E beads
- (16) Turquoise E beads
- Memory wire ring
- Chain nose pliers
- Wire cutters

Note
Memory wire loop sizes can vary, so you may use less beads than called for.

26

Variation
Add charms at the ends for a new look.

27

Faceted Crystal Choker

by SARAH STULL

Variation

Try using round glass beads for a casual look.

Step 1

String one crimp bead onto the beading wire, then thread the wire through the ring on one side of the clasp and back through the crimp bead as shown in **Diagram A** below. Crimp the bead.

Step 2

String beads onto the wire in the following order: one E bead and three tube beads. Repeat this pattern six more times.

Step 3

String additional beads onto the wire in the following order: one small crystal bead, one spacer, one small crystal bead, one E bead, one tube bead, one E bead, one spacer, one small crystal bead, one spacer, and one medium crystal bead.

Step 4

String the center filigree bead onto the wire. Repeat Steps 2 and 3, stringing the beads onto the wire in the opposite order.

Step 5

String the remaining crimp bead onto the wire, then thread the wire through the ring on the other side of the clasp and back through the crimp bead. Crimp the bead and trim off the wire ends.

Step 6

Fasten the clasp.

Shell & Coconut Bead Ankle Bracelet

by PATTY COX

You Will Need

- Natural coconut beads
- Predrilled shells
- .015" beading wire
- (2) Crimp beads
- Spring-ring clasp with jump ring
- Chain nose pliers
- Wire cutters

Step 1

Cut a length of beading wire to equal the measurement of your ankle plus 4". String one crimp bead onto the wire, then thread the wire through the ring on the clasp and back through the crimp bead as shown in **Diagram A** below. Crimp the bead.

Step 2

String five beads and one shell onto the wire.

Step 3

Repeat Step 2 to the length you need.

Step 4

String the remaining crimp bead onto the wire, then thread the wire through the jump ring on the clasp and back through the crimp bead. Crimp the bead and thread the wire ends back through several beads and shells.

Step 5

Fasten the clasp.

Variation

Use a similar pattern of beads and shells threaded onto 2" headpins, then attached to bobbie pins, to make matching hair dangles.

Beaded Teardrop Choker

by SARAH STULL

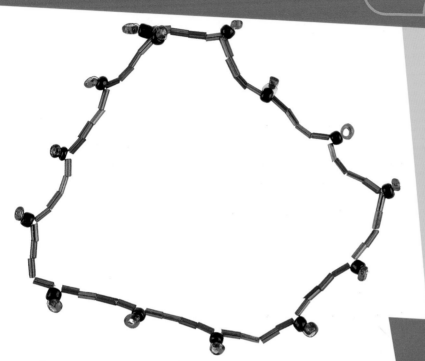

You Will Need

- Red bugle beads
- Black E beads
- Red E beads
- (22") Clear elastic cord
- Craft glue
- Tape

Note

This choker was created with elastic cord. It is important to use strong cord that will allow you to stretch the choker over your head. Test the cord first. If the cord will not stretch far enough, you will need to add a spring ring or barrel clasp.

Step 1

Tightly wrap a small piece of tape around one end of the elastic cord to keep the beads from falling off. Tie an overhand knot in the cord, just above the tape.

Step 2

String four bugle beads, one black E bead, and one red E bead onto the cord. Thread the cord back through the black E bead to form a "teardrop." The red E bead will twist so it will be at a right angle to the black E bead, as shown in **Diagram A** below.

Step 3

Repeat Step 2 to the length you need as shown in **Diagram B** below.

Step 4

Tie an overhand knot at the end of the cord and carefully remove the tape from the other end. Tie both cord ends together, using a double knot. Trim off the cord ends and place a dab of glue on the knots. Let dry.

Woven Wire Bracelet & Choker Set

by DIMPLES MUCHERINO

You Will Need

To make one bracelet:

- (27) Black opal E beads
- (½ yd.) 18-gauge melon plastic-coated wire
- (1⅓ yd.) 22-gauge copper plastic-coated wire
- Chain nose pliers
- Wire cutters

To make one matching choker:

- (63) Black opal E beads
- (28") 18-gauge melon plastic-coated wire
- (4 yds.) 22-gauge copper plastic-coated wire
- Chain nose pliers
- Wire cutters

Step 1

Bend the melon-colored wire into a "U" shape. Place the sides approximately ½" apart as shown in **Diagram A** below.

Step 2

Begin by attaching one end of the copper-colored wire to the melon-colored wire as shown in **Diagram B** below. Continuously wrap the copper-colored wire around the melon-colored wire, ending on the opposite side as shown.

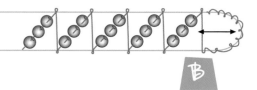

Step 3

Pull the copper-colored wire straight across to the opposite side and wrap it around the melon-colored wire once or twice as shown.

Step 4

String three beads onto the copper-colored wire, pull the wire diagonally across to the opposite side, and wrap it around the melon-colored wire once or twice as shown.

Step 5

Repeat Steps 3 and 4 to the length you need.

Step 6

Bend the end into a "U" shape and overlap the ends approximately ½" as shown in **Diagram C** below. Trim off the wire ends.

(continued on page 34)

Variation

Use different colors of wire to change the appearance of your bracelet and choker set.

Safety Pin Medallion Necklace is shown on Page 46

(continued from page 32)

Step 7

Tightly wrap the copper-colored wire around the area where the melon-colored wires overlap as shown in **Diagram D** below.

D

Step 8

Weave the remaining copper-colored wire in and out of each side at each beaded section.

Step 9

Bend the bracelet into a "C" shape.

Ladybug Illusion Choker

by PATTY COX

Step 1

String one crimp tube onto the nylon cord, then thread the cord through the ring on one side of the clasp and back through the crimp tube as shown in **Diagram A** below. Crimp the tube.

Step 2

String one more crimp tube onto the cord approximately 2" from the first one. Crimp the tube.

Step 3

String one ladybug bead onto the cord and place it against the crimp tube. String another crimp tube onto the cord and place it against the ladybug bead. Crimp the tube.

Step 4

Repeat Steps 2 and 3, every 2", to the length you need.

Step 5

String the remaining crimp tube onto the cord, then thread the cord through the ring on the other side of the clasp and back through the crimp tube. Crimp the tube and trim off the cord ends.

Step 6

Fasten the clasp.

You Will Need

- (6) Ladybug beads
- (½ yd.) Clear nylon cord
- (12) Crimp tubes
- Barrel clasp
- Chain nose pliers

Delicate Twisted Wire Bracelet & Choker Set

by DIMPLES MUCHERINO

You Will Need

To make one bracelet:

- (9) E beads in assorted colors
- (28") 24-gauge melon plastic-coated wire
- Chain nose pliers
- Wire cutters

To make one matching choker:

- (17) E beads in assorted colors
- (52") 24-gauge melon plastic-coated wire
- Chain nose pliers
- Wire cutters

Step 1

Cut the wire into one 4" length and eight 3" lengths. Bend one end of the 4" length of wire back 1³/₄"; then twist together twice, leaving a ³/₄" loop as shown in **Diagram A** below. Tightly wrap the remainder of the short wire around the straight wire, below the loop as shown.

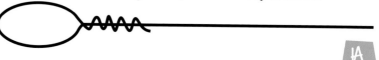

Step 2

String one bead onto the straight wire. Bend the wire back ¹/₂" from the bead, leaving a small loop on the end as shown in **Diagram B** below. Tightly wrap the remainder of the wire around the straight wire and back to the bead.

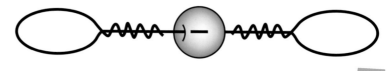

Step 3

Pinch the ³/₄" wire loop together and bend in half to form a "hook" as shown in **Diagram C** below.

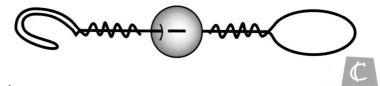

Step 4

To make the next link, insert one half of a 3" length of wire through the small loop on the first link. Bend one of the wires back, leaving a small loop on the end; then tightly wrap the remaining wire around the straight wire, below the loop and toward the center.

Step 5

String one bead onto the straight wire. Bend the wire back toward the bead, leaving a small loop on the opposite end; then tightly wrap the remaining wire around the straight wire.

36

(continued on page 38)

Variation

Adjust the length of your bracelet or choker by simply adding or removing links.

(continued from page 36)

Step 6

Repeat Steps 4 and 5 on page 36 to make the remaining seven links. Make the loop on the last link just large enough for the hook to fit through.

Step 7

Shape the bracelet into a circle and place the hook through the loop to fasten.

Chinese Coin Knot Choker

by PATTY COX

Step 1

Beginning 2" from one end of the satin cord, form a Chinese coin knot as shown in **Diagrams A and B** below.

Step 2

Place a dab of glue on each of the outside loops as shown in **Diagram C** below. Temporarily pin the loops in the cord to keep them from moving. Let dry.

Step 3

Form another Chinese coin knot and slide it next to the first one. Glue the outside loops and pin in place. Let dry.

Step 4

Repeat Step 3 to the length you need. Remove the pins.

Step 5

Trim the cord so each end measures approximately 2". Crimp the clasp onto the ends.

You Will Need

- (1½ yds.) 2mm variegated neon satin cord
- Spring-ring clasp with C-crimp
- Straight pins
- Jewelry glue
- Chain nose pliers

Variation
Try experimenting with different types of knots.

39

Braided Wire Charm Bracelet

by DIMPLES MUCHERINO

You Will Need

- Pewter heart charm
- (20") 24-gauge blue plastic-coated wire
- (20") 24-gauge pink plastic-coated wire
- (20") 24-gauge white plastic-coated wire
- Jump ring
- Chain-nose pliers
- Wire cutters

Step 1

Bend the pink-colored wire in half. Make a small loop by twisting the wire several times as shown in **Diagram A** below.

Step 2

Bend the white-colored wire in half and twist it onto the pink-colored wire, beginning below the loop as shown in **Diagram B** below.

Step 3

Repeat Step 2 with the blue-colored wire as shown in **Diagram C** below.

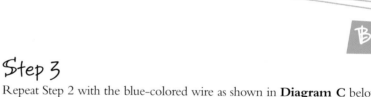

Step 4

Keep both strands of each color together. Braid the wires to the length you need, keeping them flat and untwisted.

Step 5

Trim one end of the pink-colored wire leaving 2" in length. Bend the wire in half and place the trimmed end against the braid. Trim off the remaining pink-colored wire and both white-colored wires at the end of the braid.

Step 6

Tightly wrap both of the blue-colored wires around the pink- and white-colored wires, then trim off the wire ends.

Step 7

Pinch the white-colored wire loop together and bend in half to form a "hook."

Step 8

Find the center of the braid. Open the jump ring and place it over two strands of the braided wire. Attach the heart charm and close the jump ring.

Step 9

Shape the bracelet into a circle and place the hook through the loop to fasten.

Twisted Half-square Knot Bracelet

by DIMPLES MUCHERINO

- (10) E beads in assorted colors
- (20") 22-gauge copper plastic-coated wire
- (2½ yds.) 24-gauge copper plastic-coated wire
- Chain nose pliers
- Wire cutters

Step 1

Bend one end of the 22-gauge wire back 1"; then twist together twice, leaving a small loop as shown in **Diagram A** below. Tightly wrap the remainder of the short wire around the straight wire, below the loop as shown.

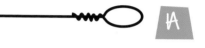

Step 2

Bend the 24-gauge wire in half and twist it onto the 22-gauge wire, beginning below the loop as shown in **Diagram B** below.

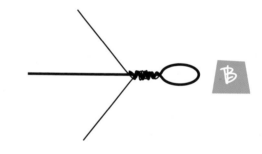

Step 3

Tie one half-square knot in the 24-gauge wire as shown in **Diagram C** below.

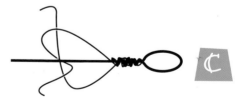

Step 4
String one bead onto the 22-gauge wire and place it below the knot. Tie five half-square knots in the 24-gauge wire.

Step 5
Repeat Step 4 to the length you need.

Step 6
Trim one end of the 22-gauge wire to 2" in length. Bend the wire in half and place the trimmed end against the last knot. Trim one of the 24-gauge wires to $\frac{1}{2}$" in length and line it up with the 22-gauge wire. Tightly wrap the remaining 24-gauge wire around the 22- and 24-gauge wires for $\frac{1}{2}$". Trim off the wire ends.

Step 7
Pinch the 22-gauge wire loop together and bend in half to form a "hook."

Step 8
Shape the bracelet into a circle and place the hook through the loop to fasten.

Variation
Use two different colors of wire to turn your bracelet into a multicolored fashion accessory.

Braided Wire Choker

by DIMPLES MUCHERINO

by DIMPLES MUCHERINO

You Will Need

- (42") 18-gauge lime green plastic-coated wire
- (42") 18-gauge silver plastic-coated wire
- (42") 18-gauge yellow plastic-coated wire
- Chain nose pliers
- Wire cutters

Step 1

Bend each wire in half and connect as shown in **Diagram A** below.

1A

Step 2

Keep both strands of each color together. Braid the wires to the length you need, keeping them flat and untwisted.

Step 3

Trim all of the wire ends to ½" in length. Bend the wires to one side.

Step 4

Shape the choker into a circle.

Variation

Shorten the braid to make a bracelet instead of a choker.

44

Safety Pin Medallion Necklace

by PATTY COX

You Will Need

- (16) 4mm gold metal beads
- (16) 4mm x 6mm tie-dyed tube beads
- (16) E beads in assorted colors
- (48) Gold seed beads
- (²/₃ yd.) Black faux-suede cord
- (8) ³/₄" gold safety pins
- (8) ⁷/₈" gold safety pins
- .015" beading wire
- (2) Gold crimp beads
- Spring-ring clasp with jump ring
- Chain nose pliers
- Wire cutters

Step 1

Open each safety pin. Place beads onto each ³/₄" safety pin in the following order: one seed bead, one tube bead, and two seed beads as shown in **Diagram A** below.

Step 2

Place beads onto each ⁷/₈" safety pin in the following order: one seed bead, one tube bead, one seed bead, one E bead, and one seed bead as shown in **Diagram B** below. Close each safety pin and pinch the top closures so they cannot open.

Step 3

Thread all of the safety pins onto the beading wire by placing the wire through the circle at the bottom of each safety pin while alternating the sizes as shown in **Diagram C** below. End with one crimp bead.

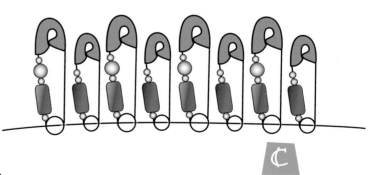

Step 4

Cut the wire, then string the crimp bead onto the opposite end of the wire. Pull the wires tightly. Crimp the bead and trim off the wire ends.

Woven Wire Choker is shown on page 45.

Step 5

Thread another length of wire through the holes in the top closures of the first safety pins, as shown in **Diagram D** below. Then place beads in between each safety pin in the following order: one seed bead, one 4mm metal bead, and one seed bead. End with the remaining crimp bead.

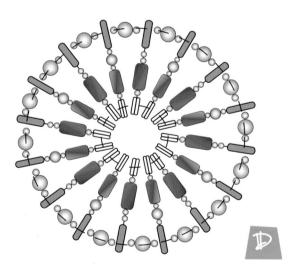

D

Variation

Try silver safety pins embellished with a single color of beads.

Step 6

Repeat Step 4 on page 46 on the outside to complete the medallion.

Step 7

Tie the faux-suede cord onto the outer edge of the medallion and attach the clasp to the ends of the cord.

Coiled Wire Choker

by DIMPLES MUCHERINO

You Will Need

- (57) Iridescent E beads
- (3") 18-gauge copper plastic-coated wire
- (½ yd.) 22-gauge copper plastic-coated wire
- (1½ yds.) 24-gauge copper plastic-coated wire
- (1½ yds.) 24-gauge gold plastic-coated wire
- Chain nose pliers
- Wire cutters

Step 1

Cut both colors of the 24-gauge lengths of wire into nine 6" lengths. Bend one end of the 22-gauge wire back 1½"; then twist together twice, leaving a ¾" loop. Tightly wrap the remainder of the short wire around the straight wire, below the loop.

Step 2

Pinch the ¾" wire loop together and bend in half to form a "hook."

Step 3

Continuously wrap one of the 6" lengths of copper-colored wire in a ½"-long spiral around the length of 18-gauge wire. Trim off the wire ends and slide the coil off the wire. Repeat until you have nine copper-colored coils and nine gold-colored coils.

Step 4

String one copper-colored coil and three E beads onto the 22-gauge wire below the hook. String another copper-colored coil and three E beads onto the wire. String one gold-colored coil and three E beads onto the wire. Repeat to the length you need, alternating the copper- and gold-colored coils. End with a copper-colored coil.

Step 5

Bend the 22-gauge wire end back ¾" from the last coil; then twist together twice, leaving a small loop just large enough for the hook to fit through.

Step 6

Tightly wrap the 22-gauge wire around itself back to the last copper-colored coil. Trim off the wire end.

Step 7

Shape the choker into a circle and place the hook through the loop to fasten.

Variation

Make two identical chokers in different lengths. Hook them together, hook to loop, and wear them as one.

Macramé Bracelet

by PATTY COX

by PATTY COX

You Will Need

- (6) 10mm x 13mm turquoise ceramic beads
- (½ yd.) .015" beading wire
- (2 yds.) 1mm hemp beading twine
- (2) Crimp beads
- Barrel clasp
- Jewelry glue
- Chain nose pliers
- Wire cutters

Step 1

String one crimp bead onto the beading wire, then thread the wire through the ring on one side of the clasp and back through the crimp bead as shown in **Diagram A** below. Crimp the bead.

Step 2

Thread the beading twine through the ring on the clasp and pull until it is centered.

Step 3

Tie five square knots in the twine, keeping the wire between each knot as shown in **Diagram B** below. String one bead onto the wire.

Step 4

Repeat Step 3 to the length you need.

Step 5

String the remaining crimp bead onto the wire, then thread the wire through the ring on the other side of the clasp and back through the crimp bead. Crimp the bead and trim off the wire ends.

Step 6

Tie the twine to the ring on the clasp, then trim off the twine ends. Place a dab of glue on the trimmed ends of the twine to keep them from fraying. Let dry.

Step 7

Fasten the clasp.

Turquoise Nugget Choker

by PATTY COX

You Will Need

- (2) 4mm silver metal beads
- Silver feather charm
- Silver seed beads
- Turquoise chip beads
- (½ yd.) .015" beading wire
- (2) Crimp beads
- Spring-ring clasp with jump ring
- Jump ring
- Chain nose pliers
- Wire cutters

Variation

For a more formal choker, use pearls.

Step 1

String one crimp bead onto the beading wire, then thread the wire through the ring on the clasp and back through the crimp bead as shown in **Diagram A** below. Crimp the bead.

Step 2

String one 4mm metal bead onto the wire and place it against the crimp bead. Keep stringing one turquoise chip and one seed bead onto the wire to the length you need. End with the remaining 4mm metal bead.

Step 3

String the remaining crimp bead onto the wire, then thread the wire through the jump ring on the clasp and back through the crimp bead. Crimp the bead and thread the wire ends back through several seed beads and turquoise chips.

Step 4

Find the center of the choker. Open the jump ring and place it between a turquoise chip and a seed bead. Attach the feather charm and close the jump ring.

Step 5

Fasten the clasp.

Faceted Crystal Chocker on left is shown on page 29.

Single-weave Beaded Bracelet

by PATTY COX

You Will Need

- (28) ⁶⁄₀ green rocaille beads
- (54) ⁶⁄₀ blue rocaille beads
- (²⁄₃ yd.) .015" beading wire
- Crimp bead
- Spring-ring clasp with jump ring
- Chain nose pliers
- Wire cutters

Step 1

Bend the beading wire into a "U" shape. String one green bead onto the wire and place it at the center of the U as shown in **Diagram A** below.

Step 2

String one blue bead onto each side of the wire, then thread each of the wires through a single green bead as shown in **Diagram B** below. Pull the wires tightly.

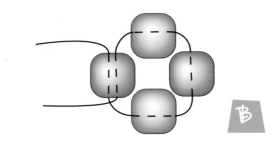

Step 3

Repeat Step 2 to the length you need. End with one green bead.

Step 4

String the crimp bead onto both wires, then thread the wires through the ring on the clasp and back through the crimp bead as shown in **Diagram C** below. Crimp the bead and thread the wire ends back through several beads.

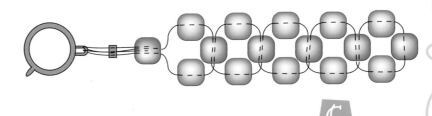

Step 5

Open the jump ring on the clasp and place it through the beginning green bead. Close the jump ring.

Step 6

Fasten the clasp.

Variation

String beads, alternating colors, onto elastic cord to make a matching ring.

Chain Stitch Charm Necklace

by PATTY COX

- (9) Flower charms
- (2½ yds.) 2mm variegated neon satin cord
- Spring-ring clasp with C-crimp
- (9) Jump rings
- Crochet hook
- Chain nose pliers

Step 1

Form a loop at one end of the satin cord as shown in **Diagram A** below.

Step 2

Place the crochet hook through the loop. Catch the long end of the cord and pull it through the loop as shown in **Diagram B** below. Pull the cords so the loop snugly fits around the neck of the hook.

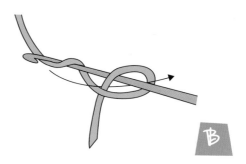

Step 3

Wrap the long end of the cord around the hook and pull it through the loop as shown in **Diagram C** below. Adjust the tension by pulling the long end of the cord and making each stitch the same size as the first one.

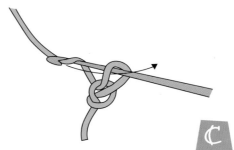

Variation

Try alphabet charms to write a word or your name.

56

Step 4
Repeat Step 3 on page 56 to the length you need. Remove the hook.

Step 5
Thread the end of the cord through the loop and pull to make a knot.
Crimp the clasp onto the ends.

Step 6
Open each jump ring and place them, evenly spaced, over the cord.
Attach the flower charms and close the jump rings. Attach flower charm
to jump ring. Then attach each to cord. Attach flower charm to jump
ring then attach each to cord.

Step 7
Fasten the clasp.

Floating Cabochon Hair Accessory

by PATTY COX

by PATTY COX

You Will Need

To make five hair accessories:

- (5) 8mm cabochons in assorted colors
- (25") 16-gauge copper wire
- Jewelry glue
- Round nose pliers
- Wire cutters

Step 1

Cut the wire into five 5" lengths. Hold the end of each length of wire with the pliers and gently bend the wire into a 1" coil.

Step 2

Apply glue to the back of each cabochon and place one in the center of each wire coil. Let dry.

Step 3

Place each coil in your hair and gently turn. The wire coil will disappear, leaving only the cabochon showing.

Variation

Use objects with at least one flat side, such as buttons or charms.

Clear Beaded Bracelet

by ALI RUSS

Step 1

Fold the nylon cord in half. Thread the folded end of the cord through the ring on one side of the clasp and tie the cords together just below the clasp, using a double knot.

Step 2

String one glass bead onto both cords. Separate the cords and string one seed bead, one bugle bead, one seed bead, one bugle bead, and one seed bead onto each length of cord.

Step 3

Bring both cords back together. Repeat Step 2 until all beads have been used. Tie both cords in a double knot.

Step 4

Thread both cords through the ring on the remaining side of the clasp and tie in a double knot.

Step 5

Fasten the clasp.

You Will Need

- (7) Clear glass beads
- (28) Silver bugle beads
- (40) Clear seeds beads
- (²/₃ yd.) Clear nylon cord
- Barrel clasp

Variation

Use beading wire instead of cord. This will create a more defined diamond shape between the glass beads.

Variegated Clay Bead Choker

by SYNDEE HOLT

You Will Need

- (1 oz.) Green polymer clay
- (1 oz.) Turquoise polymer clay
- (1 oz.) Violet polymer clay
- Wire choker with ball clasp
- Large needle
- Sheet of typing paper
- Baking sheet

Step 1
Divide each of the colors of clay into thirds. Using one portion of each color, roll the clay into long worm-shaped pieces approximately 3" in length.

Step 2
Twist all three "worms" together. Keep in mind, the more you twist, the more intricate the pattern.

Step 3
Pinch off a small piece of the multicolored clay. Roll it into a ball approximately $\frac{1}{2}$" in diameter. Then roll the ball on the outside area of your palm with your hands very flat. This will make a "football-shaped" bead. Press the two ends together.

Step 4
Repeat Step 3 until you have used up all of the multicolored clay. Pick your three favorite beads. Set the beads aside.

Variation
String the unused beads onto a length of elastic cord to make a bracelet to match.

Step 5

Using portions of the turquoise and violet clay, make four round beads from each color by rolling the clay into pea-sized balls. Set aside.

Step 6

Slowly twist the needle through the tops of each multicolored bead and through the center of each round bead to make a hole. Wash your hands.

Step 7

Place the sheet of typing paper on a baking sheet and place the clay beads on top of the paper so none of them are touching. Bake according to the directions on the packages of clay. Let cool.

Step 8

Remove the ball clasp from the choker. String clay beads onto the choker in the following order: one turquoise, one violet, one multicolored, one violet, one turquoise, one multicolored, one turquoise, one violet, one multicolored, one violet, and one turquoise. Replace the ball.

Beaded Leather Choker

by SARAH STULL

You Will Need

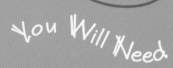

- (3) Clay beads
- (4) Silver metal beads
- (15") 2mm round black leather cord
- (2) Wire coil end caps
- Barrel clasp
- Jewelry glue
- Chain nose pliers

Step 1

Place a dab of glue on one end of the leather cord and slip on one wire coil. Crimp the wire coil. Let dry.

Step 2

String one metal bead, one clay bead, one metal bead, one clay bead, one metal bead, one clay bead, and one metal bead onto the cord.

Step 3

Place a dab of glue on the remaining end of the cord and slip on the remaining wire coil. Crimp the wire coil. Let dry.

Step 4

Pull out the last coiled loop on each wire coil and place the wire loops through the rings on each side of the clasp as shown in **Diagram A** below. Slightly crimp each loop.

A

Step 5

Fasten the clasp.

Variation

Use a color of leather cord to complement the color of the beads you are using.

62

Beaded Leather Ankle Bracelet

by SARAH STULL

You Will Need

- (2) Decorative beads
- (3) Silver metal beads
- 2mm round black leather cord
- (2) Wire coil end caps
- Barrel clasp
- Jewelry glue
- Chain nose pliers

Step 1

Cut a length of leather cord to equal the measurement of your ankle plus 4". Place a dab of glue on one end of the cord and slip on one wire coil. Crimp the wire coil. Let dry.

Step 2

String one metal bead, one decorative bead, one metal bead, one decorative bead, and one metal bead onto the cord.

Step 3

Place a dab of glue on the remaining end of the cord and slip on the remaining wire coil. Crimp the wire coil. Let dry.

Step 4

Pull out the last coiled loop on each wire coil and place the wire loops through the rings on each side of the clasp as shown in **Diagram A** below. Slightly crimp each loop.

A

Variation

Keep in mind that it is often best to use an odd number of beads so one bead will be in the center.

Step 5

Fasten the clasp.

Butterfly Earrings

by SARAH STULL

You Will Need

- (2) Silver butterfly beads
- (8) Pearlescent seed beads
- (2) Ear wires
- (2) 2" headpins with looped ends
- Round nose pliers
- Wire cutters

Variation

Use a combination of E beads and two sizes of flat, round, or clear crystal beads.

Step 1

String two seed beads, one butterfly bead, and two seed beads onto each headpin.

Step 2

For each earring, bend the headpin at a right angle as shown in **Diagram A** at right.

Step 3

Bend the headpin back in the opposite direction to form a loop as shown in **Diagram B** below. Hold the loop in the tip of the pliers and twist the wire around the bottom of the loop two times. Trim off the wire ends.

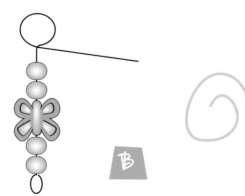

Step 4

Open the loop on one of the ear wires and attach it to one of the beaded headpins. Close the loop. Repeat for the remaining earring.

Adjustable Leather Cord Necklace

by PATTY COX

Step 1

Cut the leather cord into two equal lengths. Thread one end of one length of cord through one side hole of the charm. Fold the cord back, overlapping itself ³/₄", and attach one crimp clasp. Crimp the clasp. Repeat with one end of the remaining length of cord.

Step 2

String all three metal beads onto one cord end. Thread the remaining cord end through the beads in the opposite direction.

Step 3

Tie a knot at each cord end, using an overhand knot. Place a dab of glue on the knots. Let dry.

You Will Need

- (3) 10mm gold metal beads
- Gold open-heart charm with side holes
- (28") 2mm round black leather cord
- (2) Crimp clasps
- Jewelry glue
- Chain nose pliers

Variation

Use any open-shape charm or pendant with two holes on each side.

Beaded Circle Choker

by SARAH STULL

You Will Need

- (18) Red glass beads in assorted shapes & sizes
- (1 yd.) .015" red beading wire
- Barrel clasp
- Wire cutters

Variation
Adjust the length of your choker by simply adding or removing beads.

Step 1
Fold the beading wire in half. Thread one wire end through the ring on one side of the clasp. Thread both wire ends through one glass bead and tie in a double knot.

Step 2
Separate the wires. Thread one wire through one side of one glass bead; thread the remaining wire through the other side of the same glass bead. Leave a large loop of wire forming a circle.

Step 3
Repeat Step 2 until all beads have been used. Slide the beads until all of the loops are the same size.

Step 4
Thread both wires through the ring on the remaining side of the clasp and tie in a double knot. Trim off the wire ends.

Step 5
Fasten the clasp.

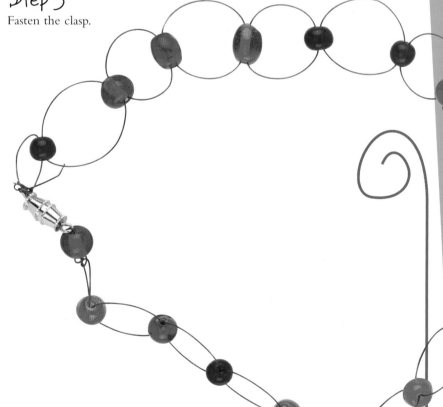

Sports Bead Necklace

by PATTY COX

Step 1

Cut the ribbon into one 16" length and one 18" length. Mark the center of each length of ribbon. Beginning at the center, measure and mark 2" sections on each side of center on both lengths of ribbon.

Step 2

String beads onto the 16" length of ribbon, beginning at the center, and place one at each mark in the following order: one soccer ball bead at the center, one black faceted bead on each side, one clear faceted bead on each side, and one black faceted bead on each side. Place a dab of glue at each bead. Let dry.

Step 3

String beads onto the 18" length of ribbon, beginning at the center, and place one at each mark in the following order: one soccer ball bead at the center, one black faceted bead on each side (positioned half way to the nearest marks), one soccer ball bead on each side, one clear faceted bead on each side, one soccer ball bead on each side, and one black faceted bead on each side. Place a dab of glue at each bead. Let dry.

Step 4

Bring both lengths of ribbon together on each end. Crimp the clasp onto the ends.

Variation

Use different sport beads such as baseball or basketball.

You Will Need

- (4) 4mm clear faceted crystal plastic beads
- (6) 12mm soccer ball beads
- (8) 4mm black faceted plastic beads
- (34") ¼"-wide red satin ribbon
- Spring-ring clasp with C-crimp
- Jewelry glue
- Marking pen
- Chain nose pliers

Simple Beaded Bracelets

by ANNA RUSS

You Will Need

To make each bracelet:
- Bugle beads in any color
- Seed beads in any color
- Flexible beading needle
- (⅓ yd.) Elastic cord
- Craft glue
- Tape

Step 1
Tightly wrap a small piece of tape around one end of the elastic cord to keep the beads from falling off. Tie an overhand knot in the cord, just above the tape.

Step 2
Thread the cord through the needle. String three seed beads and one bugle bead onto the cord.

Step 3
Repeat Step 2 to the length you need. Remove the needle.

Step 4
Tie an overhand knot at the end of the cord and carefully remove the tape from the other end. Tie both cord ends together, using a double knot. Trim off the cord ends and place a dab of glue on the knots. Let dry.

Variation
Turn your bracelet into a dramatic one by attaching three or more bracelets together with a jump ring.

Heart Charm Hair Dangles

by PATTY COX

Step 1

Cut the chain into two equal lengths. Open ten jump rings and attach a heart charm to each one. Place five of them on each length of chain by attaching each one through a link on the chain. Close the jump rings.

Step 2

String one bicone bead onto each headpin. Trim each headpin to $^3/_8$" beyond the bead. Bend each headpin to form a loop.

Step 3

Open the remaining jump rings and attach a beaded headpin to each one. Place two of them on each length of chain by attaching each one through a link on the chain. Close the jump rings.

Step 4

Insert the bobbie pin through the top jump ring.

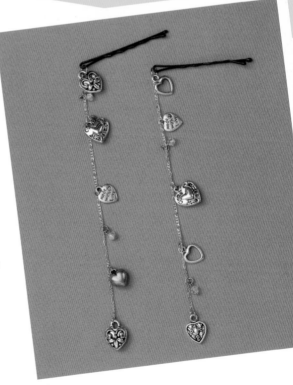

Beaded Dangle Charm Bracelet

by PATTY COX

You Will Need

- (5) Assorted silver charms
- (5) 6mm bicone beads in assorted colors
- (10) 9mm metal spacers
- (11) 4mm silver fluted metal beads
- (32) 4mm clear bicone beads
- .012" beading wire
- (2) Crimp beads
- (5) 1" headpins with flat ends
- Spring-ring clasp with jump ring
- (5) Jump rings
- Chain nose pliers
- Round nose pliers
- Wire cutters

Variation

Use pony beads or pearls to make this bracelet have a totally different look.

Step 1

String one crimp bead onto the beading wire, then thread the wire through the ring on the clasp and back through the crimp bead as shown in **Diagram A** below. Crimp the bead.

Step 2

To make dangles, string beads onto each headpin in the following order: one 4mm bicone bead, one 6mm bicone bead, and one 4mm bicone bead. Bend each headpin to form a loop.

Step 3

Attach a jump ring to each charm. Set aside.

Step 4

To make bracelet, string beads onto the beading wire in the following order: one 4mm bicone bead, one 4mm metal bead, one 4mm bicone bead, one beaded headpin, one 9mm metal spacer, one 4mm bicone bead, one 4mm metal bead, one 4mm bicone bead, one charm, and one 9mm metal spacer. Repeat this pattern four more times. End with one 4mm bicone bead, one 4mm metal bead, and one 4mm bicone bead.

Step 5

String the remaining crimp bead onto the wire, then thread the wire through the jump ring on the clasp and back through the crimp bead. Crimp the bead and thread the wire ends back through several beads.

Step 6

Fasten the clasp.

Josephine Knot & Braid Choker

by PATTY COX

You Will Need

- (2 yds.) Black rubber tubing
- Spring-ring clasp with C-crimp
- Chain nose pliers

Step 1

Cut the rubber tubing into two equal lengths. Form a loop at the center of one length of tubing as shown in **Diagram A** below.

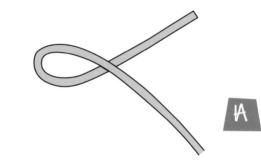

Step 2

Form a loop at the center of the remaining length of tubing and weave it around the first one as shown in **Diagram B** below.

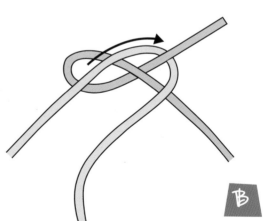

Variation

Rubber tubing is available in many colors. Make one in every color.

72

Step 3

Continue weaving the tubing over and under as shown in **Diagram C** below. Center the knot and pull the ends of the tubing to tighten.

Step 4

You will have one double strand of tubing and two single strands of tubing. Braid the strands together.

Step 5

Crimp the clasp onto the ends.

Step 6

Fasten the clasp.

Macramé Zipper Pull

by PATTY COX

You Will Need

- 20mm x 22mm orange birthstone gem
- (15) Assorted Czech E beads
- (6") .015" beading wire
- (2) Crimp beads
- 23mm lanyard hook
- 32mm split-ring key ring
- Jewelry glue
- Chain nose pliers
- Wire cutters

Variation

Make one for your backpack in colors that coordinate with it.

Step 1

String one crimp bead onto the beading wire, then thread the wire through the bottom part of the lanyard hook and back through the crimp bead as shown in **Diagram A** below. Crimp the bead.

Step 2

Cut the embroidery floss into two equal lengths. Thread both lengths of floss through the bottom part of the lanyard hook until they are centered.

Step 3

Tie one square knot in the floss, keeping the wire between the knot as shown in **Diagram B** below. String one bead onto the wire.

Step 4

Repeat Step 3 to the length you need. End with one square knot.

Step 5

String the remaining crimp bead onto the wire, then thread the wire through the key ring and the birthstone gem and back through the crimp bead. Crimp the bead and trim off the wire ends.

Step 6

Tie one last square knot in the floss, then trim off the floss ends. Place a dab of glue on the trimmed ends of the floss to keep them from fraying. Let dry.

Tumbling Dice Bracelet & Choker Set

by ANNA RUSS

You Will Need

To make one bracelet:

- (20) Translucent dice in 5 assorted colors, 4 of each color
- (95) E beads in 5 assorted colors, 19 of each color
- (3) Coils of memory wire for bracelets
- Chain nose pliers
- Wire cutters

To make one matching choker:

- (15) Translucent dice in 5 assorted colors, 3 of each color
- (75) E beads in 5 assorted colors, 15 of each color
- Memory wire choker
- Chain nose pliers
- Wire cutters

Step 1

Make a small loop at one end of the memory wire. You may need an adult to help bend the wire.

Step 2

String one die and five E beads, one of each color, onto the wire.

Step 3

Repeat Step 2, using all dice and beads. End with one die.

Step 4

Trim the remaining end of the wire, leaving ½", then make a small loop to match the loop at the opposite end of the wire.

Variation

Dice are only one style of bead; replace them with your favorite bead.

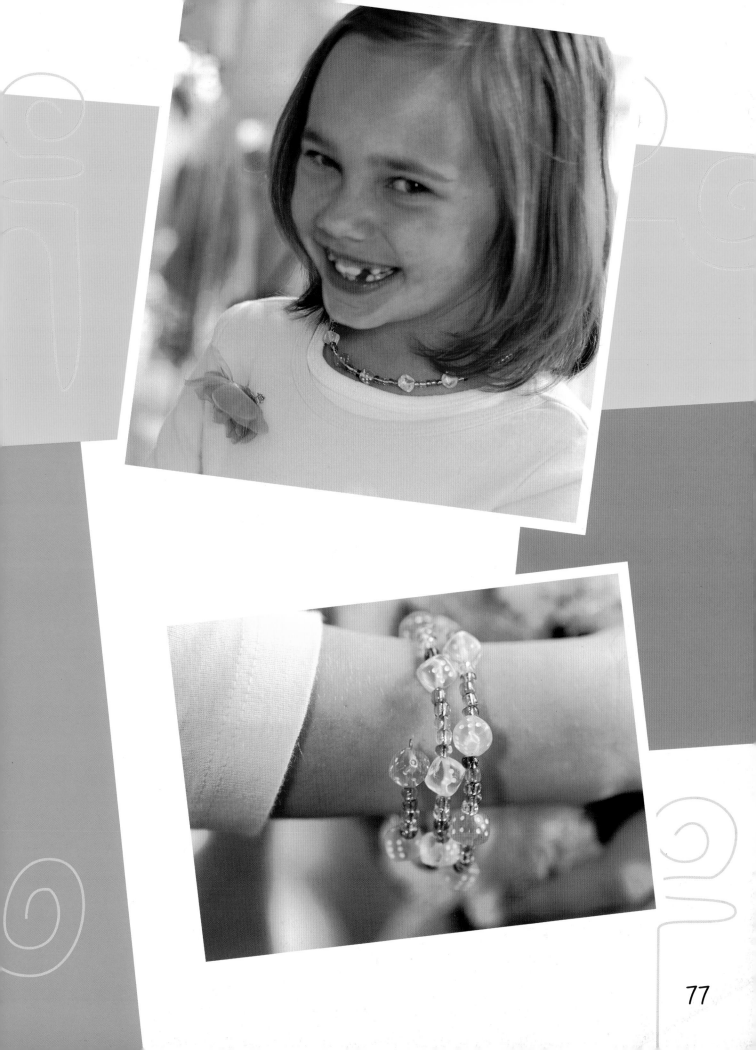

Shaped Heart Zipper Pull

by JUDY HENDRIX

You Will Need

- Pink seed beads
- White seed beads
- Small charm
- 3" square of 14-count white perforated paper
- 3" square of peel & stick white sparkle foam
- Quilting thread
- Size 10 beading needle
- (2) Jump rings
- Lobster claw clasp
- Jewelry glue
- Chain nose pliers

Step 1

In this project, you will be doing a half cross–stitch throughout the pattern. Practice coming up through hole #1, picking up a bead, and then going down diagonally into hole #2. Continue along the row as shown in **Diagram A** below.

Note: It doesn't really matter if you go from top to bottom or bottom to top, but you must always use the same slant or the bead will not lay properly. If you need to end your thread, turn to the back and run the needle under a few stitches. Trim off the thread ends.

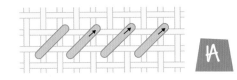

Step 2

Cut an arm's length of quilting thread. Double it and thread both cut ends through the eye of the needle.

Step 3

Beginning at the top left-hand corner, count down 15 squares and over 10 squares. Come up through the start hole as shown in **Diagram B** below, but do not pull the thread all the way through. String one pink bead onto the needle and then go diagonally across the square and down through the correct hole. Turn your work over and thread your needle through the loop of the doubled end of thread. This method will lock your first stitch into place so you will not have to tie any knots. You will do this every time you begin a new thread.

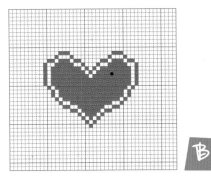

Variation

Get into the school spirit and make a zipper pull of your school emblem or mascot.

Step 4

Following **Diagram B**, bead all of the red outline first, making sure that all of the stitches are slanted in the same direction.

Step 5

Bead the white row next, all the way around. You might notice that it looks different on one side—it's okay, keep going.

Step 6

Fill in the rest of the pattern.

Step 7

To attach the charm, come up through the hole that is marked on the pattern, stitch around the loop in the charm, and go back down. Repeat this several times so that the charm is secure.

Step 8

Peel the back off of the sparkle foam and securely press it to the back of the perforated paper. Very carefully begin cutting out the heart *one square away* from the beads. At the dip in the top of the heart, leave a little extra room for the clasp.

Step 9

Open one of the jump rings. Attach it to the remaining jump ring and the clasp and close the ring. Open the jump ring that will be attached to the top of the heart and push it through the perforated paper and the foam. Close the jump ring and add a dab of glue to secure. Let dry.

Waterfall Bracelet

by ANNA RUSS

You Will Need

- (9) Blue decorative beads
- (27) Blue E beads
- (12") Elastic cord
- Craft glue
- Tape

Step 1

Tightly wrap a small piece of tape around one end of the elastic cord to keep the beads from falling off. Tie an overhand knot in the cord, just above the tape.

Step 2

String one decorative bead and three E beads onto the cord.

Step 3

Repeat Step 2 to the length you need.

Step 4

Tie an overhand knot at the end of the cord and carefully remove the tape from the other end. Tie both cord ends together, using a double knot. Trim off the cord ends and place a dab of glue on the knots. Let dry.

Variation

Use a combination of bicone, bugle, E, and faceted beads on these waterfall bracelets.

Bow Tie Bracelet

by SARAH STULL

Step 1

Thread the beading wire through the ring on one side of the clasp. Center the clasp.

Step 2

String one bugle bead onto the wire on one side of the clasp. Thread the other wire through the opposite side of the same bugle bead.

Step 3

String one bugle bead onto each wire. Bring both wires together and string one E bead onto both wires. This forms the first side of the bow tie. Separate the wires and string one bugle bead onto each wire. String one bugle bead onto one of the wires, then thread the other wire through the opposite side of the same bugle bead. The wires are now separated again and you have formed the first bow tie.

Step 4

Repeat Step 3 nine more times with the first bugle bead being the start of the next bow tie.

Step 5

Twist the wire ends together and tie an overhand knot. Thread both wires through the ring on the remaining side of the clasp and tie in a double knot. Trim off the wire ends.

Step 6

Fasten the clasp.

You Will Need

- (9) Black E beads
- (46) Blue bugle beads
- (32") .015" red beading wire
- Barrel clasp
- Wire cutters

Variation

Since the wire shows at the end of each bow tie, you can vary the color. You may also want to make the center E bead a decorative bead.

Loop Bracelet

by ALI RUSS

You Will Need

- Large silver round beads
- Small silver beads
- (24") .015" beading wire
- Barrel clasp
- Wire cutters

Step 1

Fold the beading wire in half. Thread the folded end of the wire through the ring on one side of the clasp and tie the wires together just below the clasp, using a double knot.

Step 2

String one small bead onto both wires. Separate the wires and string one large bead onto one of the wires. String five small beads onto the other wire.

Step 3

Bring both wires back together. String one small bead onto both wires. Separate the wires and string five small beads onto the top wire and one large bead onto the bottom wire. Pull the beads tightly.

82

Step 4

Bring both wires back together. Repeat Steps 2 and 3 on page 82 to
the length you need. End with one small bead strung onto both wires.
Tie both wires in a double knot.

Step 5

Thread both wires through the ring on the remaining side of the clasp
and tie in a double knot. Trim off the wire ends.

Step 6

Fasten the clasp.

Beaded Hair Clips

by ANDREA ROTHENBERG

You Will Need

- Assorted beads with large holes
- (1 yd.) Fiber of choice
- Craft glue
- Feathers
- Large bobbie pin

Step 1

Fold your fiber in half. Tie the fiber around the top piece of the bobbie pin at the open end. Lay one length of the fiber along the bobbie pin down to the rounded end. Begin winding the other fiber length around the top piece of the bobbie pin, catching the other fiber as you wind. Continue wrapping, making sure the entire top part of the pin is covered.

Step 2

Tie the two pieces of fiber together in a knot. Place a dab of glue on the knot and let dry.

Step 3

Place a bit of glue on the end of each piece of fiber and roll it between your fingers. This will make the ends stiff and pointed and it will be easier to thread on the beads. Let dry.

Step 4

Thread beads of choice onto each fiber. You can tie a knot at any point to hold the beads in different positions along the fiber.

Variations

Create these colorful and fun hair dangles to go with any outfit or to wear for a splash of color in your hair. You will never run out of ideas since you can use any fiber, floss, or yarn with any beads that have a hole large enough to pass the fiber through.

If you want, add a feather or other embellishment into the hole of the last bead and glue in place.

84

Chapter Two - Accessories

Beaded Appliqué Journal

by ANDREA ROTHENBERG

You Will Need

- Clear pony beads in assorted colors
- 11mm cubed alphabet beads (to personalize or write a saying)
- (3) Beaded flower appliqués
- (11") Beaded fringe
- Beading tray or paper plate
- Double-sided adhesive tabs
- Double-sided tape
- (1 yd.) Fiber in any color & type
- Rocaille seed beads in assorted colors
- Pearl white rocaille seed beads
- Spiral notebook with solid color cover, 9" wide x 11" long

Variation

Create your own beaded appliqué designs from paper or fabric.

Step 1

Place a strip of double-sided tape along the 11" nonspiral edge of the notebook cover. Attach the ribbon edge of the beaded fringe onto the notebook so the beads hang off the edge of the notebook.

Step 2

Place another strip of double-sided tape along the 11" nonspiral edge of the notebook cover over the ribbon edge of the beaded fringe. Make sure the ribbon edge is completely covered.

Step 3

Place the notebook over a beading tray and sprinkle multicolored seed beads onto the adhesive. Press the seed beads onto the notebook and fill in any empty spaces with additional multicolored seed beads. Save excess beads.

Step 4

Place three 2½" x 2½" squares of double-sided tape on the notebook cover as shown. Adhere one beaded flower appliqué to the center of each square. Place the notebook over the beading tray and sprinkle pearl white seed beads onto the remaining adhesive. Press the seed beads onto the notebook and fill in any empty spaces with additional pearl white seed beads.

Step 5

Place one 5" strip and one 7" strip of double-sided tape on the notebook cover as shown. Adhere each of the cubed alphabet beads, evenly spaced, to the top of the adhesive. Sprinkle multicolored seed beads onto the adhesive. Press the seed beads onto the notebook and fill in any empty spaces with additional multicolored seed beads.

Step 6

Cut the fiber into two equal lengths. Tie each length of fiber to the top of the wire spiral on the notebook. String alphabet beads onto some of the strands, placing a pony bead between each letter.

Beaded Fringe Stationery Box with Matching Pen

by PATTY COX

by PATTY COX

You Will Need

To make the pencil box:
- (¾" yd.) Beaded fringe
- Pencil box, 5" wide x 8" long
- Maroon acrylic paint
- Terra-cotta acrylic paint
- Crackle medium
- Clear acrylic spray finish
- Paintbrush
- Jewelry glue

To make the matching pen:
- Beaded fringe scraps
- (5) 6mm red bicone beads
- Ballpoint pen
- Maroon handmade paper
- (9") 16-gauge gold wire
- (3) 2" headpins with flat ends
- 2" eyepin
- Jump ring
- Jewelry glue
- Chain nose pliers
- Wire cutters

stationery box

Step 1
Paint the box with maroon. Let dry.

Step 2
Paint the box with crackle medium. Let dry.

Step 3
Paint the box with terra-cotta, using long even strokes. The paint will begin to "crack" as it dries. Let dry.

Step 4
Spray the box with acrylic spray finish. Let dry.

Step 5
Apply glue to the back of the ribbon edge of the beaded fringe and attach around the top edge of the box. Let dry and trim off the excess.

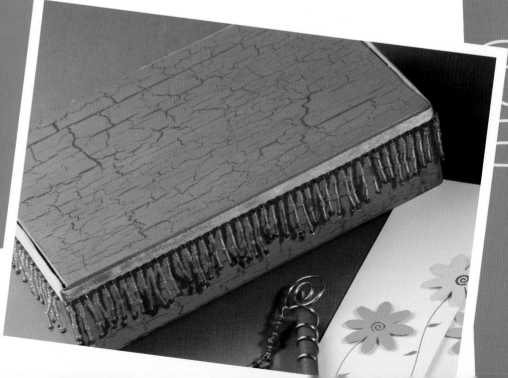

matching pen

Step 1

Wrap the ballpoint pen with the handmade paper and glue in place.

Step 2

Form a circle approximately ¹/₂" in diameter in one end of the wire. Place the pen inside the circle and adjust the size if necessary. Continue to wrap the wire around the pen two or three times. Remove the pen.

Step 3

Form a coil approximately 1" in diameter in the remaining end of the wire.

Step 4

String beads from the beaded fringe onto the eyepin along with two bicone beads.

Step 5

String beads from the beaded fringe onto each headpin along with one bicone bead.

Step 6

Attach the beaded headpins to the eyepin with a jump ring and slide the eyepin onto the wire coil. Place the pen inside the wire wrap so the beads dangle downward.

Variation

You can eliminate covering the pen with handmade paper if you have a pretty pen.

Beaded Leather Cord Bookmark

by PATTY COX

You Will Need

- (4) 10mm yellow-green ceramic beads
- (8) 4mm green glass beads
- (8) 8mm green glass beads
- (11") 2mm round black leather cord
- (2) 2" eyepins
- (2) 2" headpins with flat ends
- (2) Crimp tabs
- (4) Jump rings
- (8) 5mm washer spacers
- Chain nose pliers
- Round nose pliers

Step 1

Place one crimp tab at each end of the leather cord. Crimp the tabs.

Step 2

String the beads onto each eyepin and each headpin in the following order: one 4mm glass bead, one 8mm glass bead, one washer spacer, one 10mm ceramic bead, one washer spacer, one 8mm glass bead, and one 4mm glass bead. Bend each end of each eyepin and each headpin to form a loop.

Step 3

Attach one beaded headpin to one crimp tab with a jump ring. Attach one beaded eyepin to the remaining crimp tab with a jump ring. Attach the remaining beaded eyepin and the remaining beaded headpin to the first beaded eyepin with jump rings.

Variation

Match your bead pattern to your favorite colors.

Personalized Bookmark

by PATTY COX

Step 1

Fold one end of the satin cord over 2" and tie an overhand knot to form a small loop. Trim off the cord end close to the knot. Place a dab of glue on the trimmed end of the cord to keep it from fraying. Let dry.

Step 2

Tightly wrap a small piece of tape around the remaining end of the cord. String the alphabet beads onto the cord to spell the name of your choosing and tie an overhand knot near the last bead.

Step 3

Tie an overhand knot approximately 10" from the last knot. String additional beads onto the cord to spell the same name and tie another overhand knot near the last bead.

Step 4

Tie an overhand knot approximately 2" from the last knot. String the faceted beads onto the cord. Carefully remove the tape.

Step 5

Repeat Step 1 with the remaining end of the cord.

You Will Need

- Alphabet beads in assorted colors
- (3) 10mm faceted crystal beads in assorted colors
- (1 yd.) 2mm variegated neon satin cord
- Craft glue
- Tape

Variation

To make the perfect gift, add a gift certificate to your favorite bookstore.

Beaded Acetate Bookmark

by ANDREA ROTHENBERG

You Will Need

- Pony beads in assorted colors
- (2) Acetate strips, 2½" wide x 7" long
- Bookmark embellishments: photos, stickers, etc.
- Piece of cardstock, 1¾" wide x 6" long
- ⅛" dia. circle punch
- Craft glue
- Double-sided adhesive tabs
- (3 yds.) Embroidery floss in any color
- Marker
- Ruler

Step 1

Place the two acetate strips on top of each other, lining up the edges. Make a mark at each corner approximately ⅛" from the outside edges. Make a mark every ½" down each side and across the top and bottom approximately ⅛" from the outside edges. Using the circle punch, punch a hole at each mark.

Step 2

Lay out and attach the embellishments on top of the cardstock. Center the embellished cardstock on one of the acetate strips and secure in place with double-sided adhesive tabs. Place the remaining acetate strip on top of the one with the cardstock strip, lining up the punched holes.

Step 3

Cut the embroidery floss into three equal lengths. Place a dab of glue on each of the ends and work it in with your fingers so the ends will be pointed and dry stiff like a needle. Let dry.

Step 4

Beginning at one of the bottom corners, thread one of the lengths of floss through the aligned holes, leaving a 6" tail hanging downward. Tie an overhand knot.

Step 5

Begin "sewing" the acetate strips together, coming up through the first aligned holes, around the outside edge, and back up through the next aligned holes. Continue until you are back to the corner where you began. Tie the extra floss and the 6" tail in an overhand knot. Trim off the floss ends.

Variation
Experiment with different folders, ribbons, and trims.

Step 6

Cut the remaining lengths of floss into 12" lengths until there are
enough to go through the punched holes along the bottom of the
bookmark. Place a dab of glue on each of the ends and work it in with
your fingers as in Step 3 on page 94. Let dry.

Step 7

Thread each of the lengths of floss through the holes along the bottom
of the bookmark and pull until each side is the same length. Tie a
double knot.

Step 8

String a random number of beads onto each length of floss and tie a
double knot. String a random number of additional beads onto each
length of floss and tie another double knot. Trim off the floss ends just
past the dried glue.

Beaded Flower Garden Desk Set

by ANDREA ROTHENBERG

You Will Need

- 6mm green clear faceted crystal plastic beads (1 per flower)
- 18mm clear sunburst beads in assorted colors (4 per flower)
- 24-gauge lime green plastic-coated wire
- Metal mesh desk set
- Wire cutters
- Wooden skewer

Step 1

To create each flower, string one faceted bead onto the center of one 6" length of wire. Bend the wire in half, holding the bead in your fingers. Thread both wire ends through the hole in a sunburst bead. Pull until the faceted bead is positioned at the center of the sunburst bead.

Step 2

Determine the position of the flowers on the mesh desk accessories; they can be placed alone or in clusters. Thread the wire ends through two side-by-side holes in the mesh. Pull until the flower firmly rests against the mesh. Twist the wire ends together twice on the inside of the desk accessory. Thread the wire ends back through the holes in the mesh, positioned at each side of each flower.

Step 3

Wrap each wire end around a wooden skewer to coil.

Variation

To make drawer pulls or handles, use 25mm sunburst beads. They are larger and easier to hold on to.

Fleece Pillow with Beaded Trim

by PATTY COX

You Will Need

- 6mm x 9mm pearlescent pony beads in assorted colors
- (2) 12" x 12" squares of fleece fabric
- Polyester batting
- Masking tape
- Paper clip
- Ruler

Step 1

Place the squares of fleece fabric, right sides out, on top of each other. Measure and mark a 1½" border all the way around the squares with masking tape.

Step 2

Cut away each of the corners. Cut the fabric through both layers every ¼" and up to the masking tape border.

Step 3

Straighten one end of a paper clip to use as a tool to push the fabric fringe through the beads. String one pony bead onto each double-layered fringe. Repeat until the fringe is beaded on three sides.

Step 4

Stuff the pillow with batting and continue beading the fringe until the fourth side is complete.

Variation

Change the shape from
square to round.

Beaded Accent Trinket Box

by PATTY COX

You Will Need

- (17") Beaded fringe
- (8") Lime green eyelash fringe braid
- (2) 2" headpins with flat ends
- Lime green acrylic paint
- Violet pearl acrylic paint
- 5" dia. round papier-mâché box with lid
- (5) 1" dia. wooden doll heads
- Craft glue
- Paintbrush
- Round nose pliers

Step 1

Paint the box and lid with violet pearl. Let dry.

Step 2

Paint the wooden doll heads with lime green for the handle and the feet. Let dry.

Step 3

Place the lid on the box and draw a pencil line around the box along the bottom edge of the lid. Remove the lid.

Step 4

Apply glue to the back of the ribbon edge of the beaded fringe and attach around the box. Line up the bottom edge of the ribbon with the pencil line. Let dry and trim off the beaded fringe.

Step 5

Glue the four feet to the bottom of the box. Glue the handle to the top center of the lid. Let dry.

Step 6

Cut some beads off the extra beaded fringe and string the beads onto the headpins. Bend each headpin to form a loop.

Step 7

String the beaded headpins onto the fringe braid and glue around the handle. Let dry.

Beaded Wire Lampshade

by ANDREA ROTHENBERG

by ANDREA ROTHENBERG

You Will Need

- E beads in assorted colors
- Glass beads in assorted colors, shapes & sizes
- 22-gauge black plastic-coated wire
- Lamp with lampshade
- Tape measure
- Thin nail
- Chain nose pliers
- Wire cutters

Step 1

Note: You may want to have an adult help you with this step. Make a mark every 2" along the bottom edge of the lampshade, just above the metal edge. You may have to adjust the placement of the last hole depending on the size of the lampshade. Using the thin nail, very carefully poke a hole through the lampshade at each mark.

Step 2

Place the lampshade on the lamp. Count the number of holes and cut a 12" length of wire for each one. Bend each wire in half and insert one wire through each hole along the bottom of the lampshade.

(continued on page 104)

(continued from page 102)

Step 3

Each of the beaded dangles is made by bending the wire and threading on different beads. Begin on one side by bending the wire into a few zigzags with either your fingers or pliers, threading on some beads, then making a few more bends and curls. You can even bend the end into a large swirl. Make each one a little different, using **Diagrams A-D** below as examples. Make sure that at the end of each wire is some sort of loop so that none of the beads will fall off.

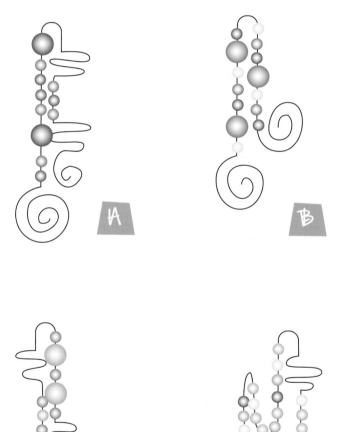

Step 4

Cut a length of wire to wrap around the base of the lamp. Place as desired and twist the wires together. Randomly bend each wire end and add beads as in Step 3.

Beaded Fringe Lampshade

by PATTY COX

Step 1

Apply glue around the bottom edge of the lampshade and attach the ribbon edge of the beaded fringe. Let dry and trim off any excess.

Step 2

Apply glue around the lampshade along the top of the ribbon edge of the beaded fringe and attach the fringe braid. Let dry and trim off any excess.

Step 3

Place the lampshade on the candle light.

You Will Need

- (½ yd.) Beaded fringe
- (½ yd.) Cranberry eyelash fringe braid
- Electric candle light
- Lampshade, 5" wide x 4" tall
- Jewelry glue

Variation

Beaded fringe can be added to any size or color lampshade. It can also be added around the top edge.

Beaded Dangle Cosmetic Bag

by PATTY COX

You Will Need

- Beads in assorted colors, sizes and types
- Beaded fringe
- Cosmetic bag with zipper
- (3) 2" eyepins
- (4) Jump rings
- Jewelry glue
- Round nose pliers

Step 1

Measure the length of the cosmetic bag zipper and cut two lengths from the beaded fringe.

Step 2

Apply glue to the back of the ribbon edge of the lengths of beaded fringe and attach to the cosmetic bag at each side of the zipper so the beads dangle downward over the ribbon.

Step 3

If the cosmetic bag has a side pocket, measure and cut a length from the beaded fringe and attach along the top inside edge of the pocket.

Step 4

Using the beads from any remaining beaded fringe combined with an assortment of additional beads, string onto the eyepins as desired. Bend each end of each eyepin to form a loop.

Step 5

To make the zipper pull, attach each beaded eyepin together with a jump ring. Attach a larger bead to one end of the zipper pull with a jump ring. Attach the remaining end to the zipper on the cosmetic bag with a jump ring.

Variation

The amount of trim needed will vary depending on the size and shape of your cosmetic bag.

Rhinestone Flip-flops

by JUDY HENDRIX

You Will Need

- 4mm flat-backed plastic rhinestones in assorted colors
- Pair of flip-flops with rubber straps
- Clear-drying industrial-strength glue
- Craft stick
- Toothpick
- Beeswax

Step 1
Turn all of the rhinestones right side up.

Step 2
Decide on a beading pattern for the straps of your flip-flops. You will begin at the center and go down each side.

Step 3
Place a small amount of beeswax on the end of a toothpick. If necessary, warm the beeswax in your fingers to make it pliable. Apply glue in small sections to one of the straps. Using the toothpick as a pick-up tool, pick up each rhinestone, one at a time, and place it in the glue. *Note: You do not want the rhinestones to be swimming in the glue, but you need enough for them to stay in place.*

Step 4
Repeat Step 3 for the remaining strap.

Step 5
Repeat Steps 3 and 4 for the remaining flip-flop. Let dry for 24 hours.

Variation
Instead of a random pattern, make flowers with the rhinestones.

Acknowledgments

Editor - Cathy Sexton
Copyeditor - Marilyn Goff
Book Design - Matt Shay
Photographer - Ryne Hazen, Zak Williams
Photo Stylist - Kim Monkres
Models - Amber Monsen, Cassidee Cunningham, Karli Moser, Kylee Cazier, Moki Sedweholm, Rachel Stoeckl, Sage Hadley

Project Designers - Patty Cox, Judy Hendrix, Syndee Holt, Dimples Mucherino, Andrea Rothenberg, Ali Russ, Anna Russ, Kristine Russ, Katherine Stull, Sarah Stull
Basic Supplies - Katherine Lamancusa
Basic Instructions - Katie Hacker

Resources:

Beadalon
205 Carter Drive
Westchester, PA 19382
www.beadalon.com

Gütermann of America, Inc.
8227 Arrowridge Blvd.
Charlotte, NC 28241
www.gutermann.com

Westrim Crafts
7855 Hayvenhurst Avenue
Van Nuys, CA 91406
1-800-727-2727

Fire Mountain Gems and Beads
One Fire Mountain Way
Grants Pass, OR 07526
1-800-355-2137
www.firemountaingems.com

Toner Plastics, Inc.
699 Silver Street
Agawan, MA 01001
1-800-723-1792
www.tonerplastics.com

Metric Equivalency Chart

inches to millimeters and centimeters

inches	mm	cm	inches	cm	inches	cm
⅛	3	0.3	9	22.9	30	76.2
¼	6	0.6	10	25.4	31	78.7
½	13	1.3	12	30.5	33	83.8
⅝	16	1.6	13	33.0	34	86.4
¾	19	1.9	14	35.6	35	88.9
⅞	22	2.2	15	38.1	36	91.4
1	25	2.5	16	40.6	37	94.0
1¼	32	3.2	17	43.2	38	96.5
1½	38	3.8	18	45.7	39	99.1
1¾	44	4.4	19	48.3	40	101.6
2	51	5.1	20	50.8	41	104.1
2½	64	6.4	21	53.3	42	106.7
3	76	7.6	22	55.9	43	109.2
3½	89	8.9	23	58.4	44	111.8
4	102	10.2	24	61.0	45	114.3
4½	114	11.4	25	63.5	46	116.8
5	127	12.7	26	66.0	47	119.4
6	152	15.2	27	68.6	48	121.9
7	178	17.8	28	71.1	49	124.5
8	203	20.3	29	73.7	50	127.0

yards to meters

yards	meters	yards	meters	yards	meters	yards	meters	yards	meters
⅛	0.11	2⅛	1.94	4⅛	3.77	6⅛	5.60	8⅛	7.43
⅛	0.11	2⅛	1.94	4⅛	3.77	6⅛	5.60	8⅛	7.43
¼	0.23	2¼	2.06	4¼	3.89	6¼	5.72	8¼	7.54
⅜	0.34	2⅜	2.17	4⅜	4.00	6⅜	5.83	8⅜	7.66
⅝	0.46	2½	2.29	4½	4.11	6½	5.94	8½	7.77
⅝	0.57	2⅝	2.40	4⅝	4.23	6⅝	6.06	8⅝	7.89
¾	0.69	2¾	2.51	4¾	4.34	6¾	6.17	8¾	8.00
⅞	0.80	2⅞	2.63	4⅞	4.46	6⅞	6.29	8⅞	8.12
1	0.91	3	2.74	5	4.57	7	6.40	9	8.23
1¼	1.03	3¼	2.86	5⅛	4.69	7¼	6.52	9⅛	8.34
1¼	1.14	3¼	2.97	5¼	4.80	7¼	6.63	9¼	8.46
1⅜	1.26	3⅜	3.09	5⅜	4.91	7⅜	6.74	9⅜	8.57
1½	1.37	3½	3.20	5½	5.03	7½	6.86	9½	8.69
1⅝	1.49	3⅝	3.31	5⅝	5.14	7⅝	6.97	9⅝	8.80
1¾	1.60	3¾	3.43	5¾	5.26	7¾	7.09	9¾	8.92
1⅞	1.71	3⅞	3.54	5⅞	5.37	7⅞	7.20	9⅞	9.03
2	1.83	4	3.66	6	5.49	8	7.32	10	9.14

Producer is the more accurate title for Kathrine Stull, the author of this second title in the 20-minute Hands On Crafts for Kids™ series. Her role is to find talented designers that follow the Hands On philosophy: "All Kids are Creative." The Hands On books are an outgrowth of the Hands On television programs, broadcast nationally on Public Television and numerous cable systems, plus as direct curriculum broadcast in the schools in over half of the country. The Hands On concept is also supported at craftsforkids.com. Her goal is providing fun and educational activities for kids.

Kathie is the president of KS Productions, one of the most prolific production companies supplying top-ranked, how-to programming to Public Television. Her shows included: *Hands On Crafts for Kids; Scrapbook Memories; Beads, Baubles, and Jewels; America Sews; America Quilts; and Needle Arts Studio*. Hands On is her flagship program dedicated to introducing kids to their creative side. Children learn in many different ways; hands-on activities play a key role in learning. Crafts are seen not only as an activity, but also as a way to build self-esteem and develop the creative spirit found in *all* children.

As a mother of three, Kathie recognizes the need for fun activities in the home and classroom where every child can be successful. She is a past board member of the Association of Craft and Creative Industries, past chair of National Craft Month, Education Committee cochair for the Craft and Hobby Association and board member of Adventures in the Arts—a program to bring arts and crafts to inner-city children.

Index